There's A MOUSE *in My* HOUSE!

Text by
SHEREE FITCH

Illustrations by
LESLIE ELIZABETH
WATTS

FIREFLY BOOKS

A FIREFLY BOOK

Published by Firefly Books Ltd. 1999

First Printing

Cataloguing in Publication Data
Fitch, Sheree
   There's a mouse in my house!
Poems.
ISBN 1-55209-392-1(bound); ISBN 0-55209-393-X (pbk)

I. Watts, Leslie Elizabeth, 1961–   .   II. Title.

PS8561.I86T43 1999   jC811'.54   C98-932857-0
PR9199.3.F57T43 1999

Published in the United States in 1999 by
Firefly Books (U.S.) Inc.
P.O. Box 1338, Ellicott Station
Buffalo, New York
14205

Author photos by Paul Darrow (S. Fitch) and Joan Watts (L.E. Watts)
Text, cover and jacket design by Avril Orloff
Printed and bound in Canada

To Jordan & Dustin, again
From kids & mice, to fine young men
   Love, Mum
   XOXO

For Emily & Stefan & their teacher,
Wilma Shannon
   Leslie

There was a mouse in our house
I guess it came in from the cold
My mother got hysterical
(And SHE'S thirty-six years old!)

Never have I witnessed
Such behavior in my life
Coming from my mother
(She's a teacher and a wife)

She yelled, she screamed, she hollered
She jumped upon the bed
"CALL ME WHEN IT'S GONE
WHEN IT'S KAPUT, WHEN IT IS DEAD!"

My mother hated violence
She'd taught me not to hit
She always said to count to ten
When in a hissy-fit

So I stood there in the kitchen
Sort of wondering what to do
Could I terminate that varmint?
Could I mash it with a shoe?

Then a trembling voice said timidly:
"H ... h ... how are you?

"I didn't mean to start a ruckus
On such a splendid day
May I say you look quite spiffy
In a human sort of way?

"I'm so sorry about your mother
You know, I've got one too
And you should see what she does
When she catches sight of you!"

That little mouse had whiskers
Fine as feathery spaghetti
She blinked her brown eyes up at me
But I kept my own gaze steady

See ...
I knew I had a job to do
And so I s l o w l y
Raised
        my
            shoe ...

I said,
"A rodent giving compliments
Is a little bit suspicious."
"Wait!" she hollered up at me
"What about my last three wishes?

"Don't you ever read?" she asked
"Don't you know just how it's done?
If I'm going to be a goner
I'm allowed to have some fun."

"Oh, please," I said. "Give me a break
This is just a stall for time
Let's get this over quickly
Without reason, without rhyme."

"But you have to grant me three last things
Before you grind my bones to dust
According to the charter
It's a mouse's right, and just."

I couldn't quibble with her logic
I'd read enough to know
That was certainly tradition
Before an execution, so ...

"What are your requests?" I asked
As she jumped into my hand

"Mmmm ...
A glass of pop, a piece of cheese
AND a chance ...
To tell you how I got here
The story of my life
My personal confession
It's a history filled with strife."

"HAVE YOU DONE IT? HAVE YOU ASKED YET?
HAVE YOU ASKED IF WE CAN STAY?"
Called her mother from the basement
"SAY WE'LL FIND A WAY TO PAY!"

So ...

I had a look inside the fridge
(The mouse got apple juice instead)
You know I think it did
A little damage to her head

She first began to hiccup
And laugh a bit too much
And then she started telling me
About her life and such

"I'll begin at the beginning
Of my genealogy
I'm extremely well connected
In fact — almost royalty

"You've heard of my three cousins?
The ones who lived inside the clock?
That's right, their names are Hickory
And Dickory and Dock

"When they got old — you guessed it —
They became the three blind mice
(I'll never forgive that farmer's wife
For cutting their tails off with a knife)"

I think she thought I'd fall for it
But I knew how tall the tale
Still, that mouse was on a roll
So I gave her ginger ale

She giggled as she burped and said,
"This cheese is rather stale."

She dribbled as she nibbled
With cheeks bulging out with cheese
But that didn't stop her talking
"Now I'll continue, if you please ...

"Great-grandpa lived in the capital
In the Parliamentary House
I'm the fourth proud generation
Of that Confederation mouse

"My grand'mère came from Old Québec
When Old Québec was young
She met her darling fiancé
In a pile of horse's dung."

I tried to interrupt her then
She'd finished all her cheese
I thought, this could go on forever
If she's doing family trees

"HAVE YOU DONE IT? HAVE YOU KILLED IT?
HAVE YOU RID US OF THE RODENT?"
It was my mother from her bedroom
"No, I haven't! Just a moment!"

But that chatting mouse continued
Feeling more and more at ease
As I got out the ricotta
AND the mozzarella cheese

"My best, most touching story
Is about my mum and dad
Have you got a lot of Kleenex?
'Cause this tale will make you sad

"When I was just a baby
My poor father lost his job
So we moved into the city
Now that's enough to make you sob

"We lived there in a high-rise
My mother hated heights
My father found some subway work
But mostly he worked nights

"It wasn't long before my mother
Said she'd had ENOUGH!
So we packed up our belongings
And that's when things got rough."

"HAVE YOU DONE IT?
HAVE YOU ASKED YET?
HAVE YOU ASKED IF WE CAN STAY?"
It was her mother from the basement
"SAY WE'LL FIND A WAY TO PAY!"

The mouse scratched her whiskers
   thoughtfully
And gabbled on and on to me ...

   "So we moved out to the country
   We had some cousins there
   There was lots of food and lots of fun
   No smog, just good clean air

   "My older sister fell in love
   She got married in the spring
   My mother looked so beautiful
   And I was asked to sing

   "In the middle of the wedding
   Some cats came on the scene
   Things after that get blurry
   Those cats were more than mean

   "We scurried off for cover
   As they pounced and hissed and spat
   I saw my pa put up his paws
   To fight the biggest cat

   "I hid inside a bucket
   Peeked out in time to see
   A dog come in the barnyard door ...

"It was CAT-astrophe!"

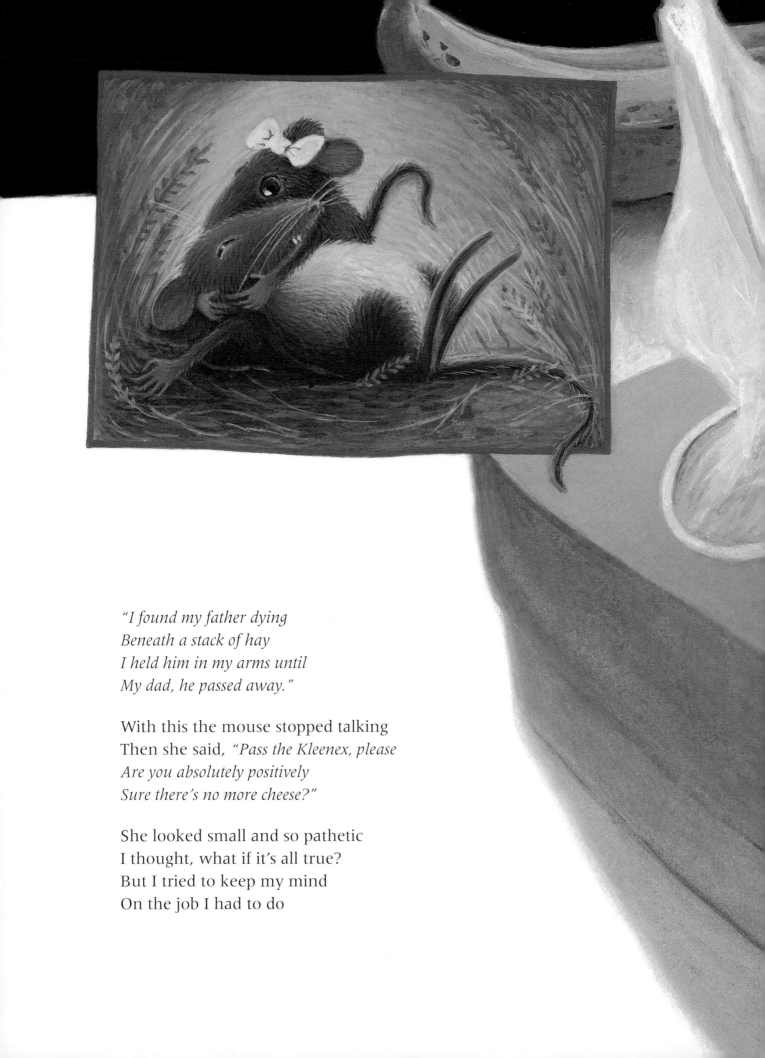

"I found my father dying
Beneath a stack of hay
I held him in my arms until
My dad, he passed away."

With this the mouse stopped talking
Then she said, "Pass the Kleenex, please
Are you absolutely positively
Sure there's no more cheese?"

She looked small and so pathetic
I thought, what if it's all true?
But I tried to keep my mind
On the job I had to do

"HAVE YOU DONE IT?"
  "HAVE YOU DONE IT?"
"HAVE YOU KILLED IT?"
  "HAVE YOU ASKED YET?"
"HAVE YOU RID US OF THE RODENT?"
  "HAVE YOU ASKED IF WE CAN STAY?"

It was our mothers both together
"Just a moment!" we replied.

Like rivers down her cheeks
That mouse's tears were slowly flowing
The sad sound of her sobbing
The hankie-honk of her nose blowing

"My sister she was widowed
Before she was a bride
Her fiancé said, Je t'aime ma femme
Just before he died

"Well ...
My sister stayed behind
So there was just my mum and me
My mother said we must be strong
In the face of tragedy

"So we headed for the mountain
We scaled the highest peak
We camped in ice and snow
There were days we didn't squeak

"Then we went to China
Then we went to Rome
We ended up in Norway
We kept trying to find a home

We just arrived here yesterday
Flew in from Copenhagen
We hitched a ride to your house
In your father's station wagon

"This is all by way of saying
We really like it here
We were thinking we'd be staying
At least until next year?

"My mother says it's finally time
To put down roots and rest
How about it? Could we make
Your home our winter nest?"

Well …

I never should have let her
Begin to tell her story
Knowing what I had to do
I said, "I'm sincerely, truly sorry, but …
You are going
                    to have
                            to die."

(I found it very difficult
To look her in the eye)
Once again I   s l o w l y
Raised
            my
                  shoe

And said, "It's going to hurt me
A whole lot more than it hurts you."

"What an incredibly illogical
Insidious line of thinking
You mean old rotten human being
Your reasoning is stinking

"Just pause a moment, meditate
Think how horrible a crime
How you will have to live with guilt
For an eternity of time

"Can you imagine for a moment
What it's like without a home?
To be cold and always hungry
In the dark and all alone?

"It seems you live in luxury
You have lots of cheese to spare
Would it really make a difference
If my mum and me lived here?"

At that moment my mum hollered
"DO YOU THINK THE COAST IS CLEAR???"

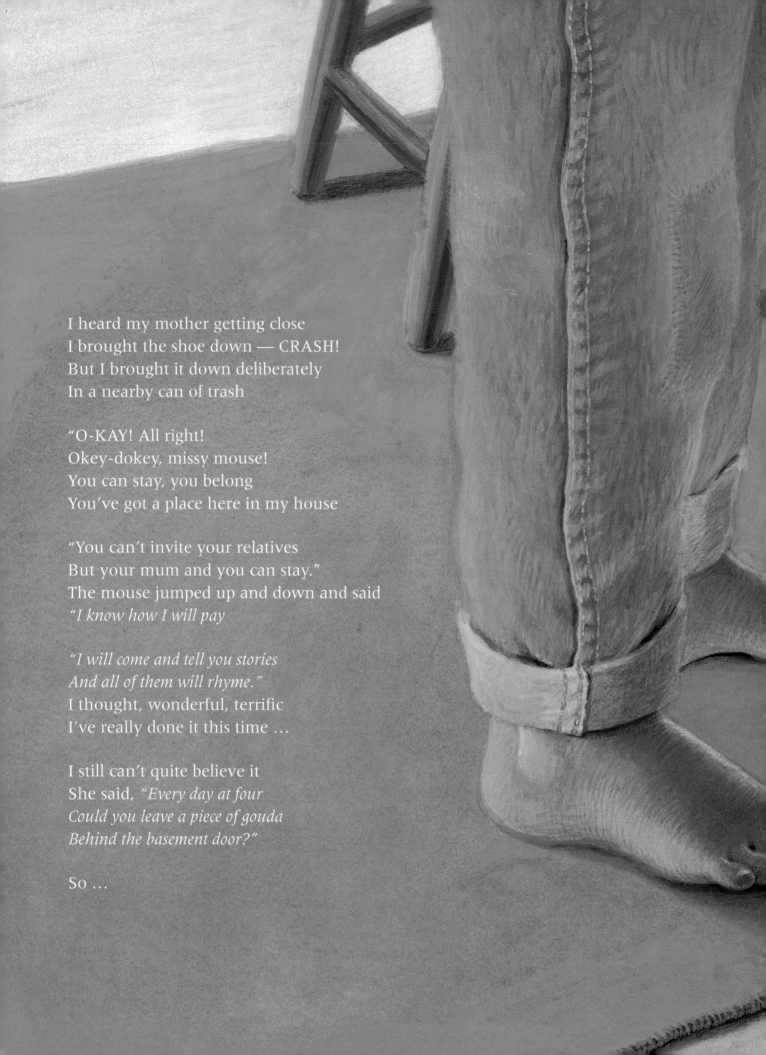

I heard my mother getting close
I brought the shoe down — CRASH!
But I brought it down deliberately
In a nearby can of trash

"O-KAY! All right!
Okey-dokey, missy mouse!
You can stay, you belong
You've got a place here in my house

"You can't invite your relatives
But your mum and you can stay."
The mouse jumped up and down and said
"I know how I will pay

"I will come and tell you stories
And all of them will rhyme."
I thought, wonderful, terrific
I've really done it this time …

I still can't quite believe it
She said, *"Every day at four*
Could you leave a piece of gouda
Behind the basement door?"

So …

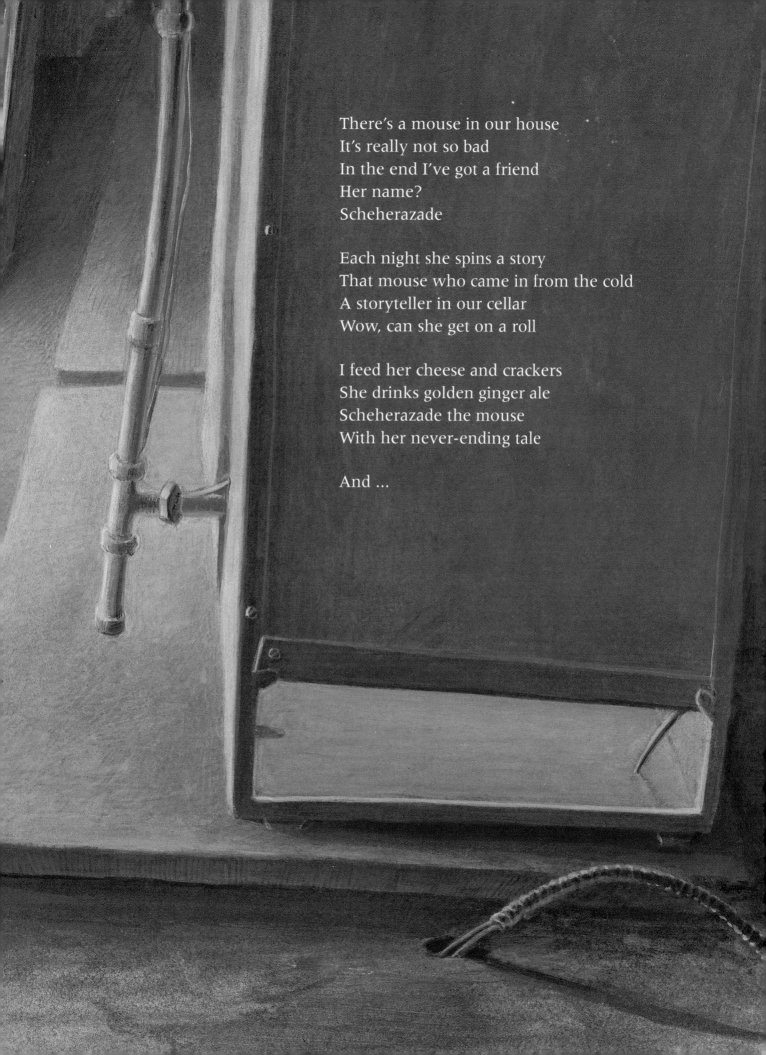

There's a mouse in our house
It's really not so bad
In the end I've got a friend
Her name?
Scheherazade

Each night she spins a story
That mouse who came in from the cold
A storyteller in our cellar
Wow, can she get on a roll

I feed her cheese and crackers
She drinks golden ginger ale
Scheherazade the mouse
With her never-ending tale

And ...

She's even taught me how to tell
Some stories of my own
She says as long as we have stories
We will never be alone

Tales of the ArabianNights